THE FOUNDATIONS

The Foundations

Simple Lessons for the New Christian to Lay a Good Foundation.

HOWARD SANDS

Sands Rodway Trust

Copyright © 1994- 2023 by Howard Sands

All rights reserved. No part of this book may be reproduced in any manner whatsoever without written permission except in the case of brief quotations embodied in critical articles and reviews.

The Foundations: Simple lessons for the New Christian to Lay a Good Foundation.

ISBN-13: 978-0-6453245-2-5 print
ISBN-10: 978-0-6453245-3-2 e-book

Apart from any fair dealing for the purposes of private study, research, criticism or review as permitted under the copyright act, no part may be reproduced by any process without the written permission of the publisher.

Publisher: **Sands Rodway Trust**
For Bulk orders for your church/organisation/group see Facebook:
https://www.facebook.com/BeautifulFeetTaskForce/shop

Books by Howard Sands
Available on All Author.
https://allauthor.com/author/howardsands/

Bible quotations used in this book are taken predominantly from the New International Version (NIV) © 1984 and the King James Version (KJV) other versions as noted.

Scripture taken from the HOLY BIBLE, NEW INTERNATIONAL VERSION®. Copyright © 1973, 1978, 1984 Biblica. Used by permission of Zondervan. All rights reserved. The "NIV" and "New International Version" trademarks are registered in the United States Patent and Trademark Office by Biblica.

First Printing, Ingram Spark Production 2023

CONTENTS

FORWARD	1
INTRODUCTION	3
THE FOUNDATIONS	4
LESSON 1 COMING TO CHRIST	5
REVIEW LESSON 1	11
LESSON 2 THE WORD OF GOD	13
REVIEW LESSON 2	17
LESSON 3 PRAYER	19
REVIEW LESSON 3	25

CONTENTS

LESSON 4 VICTORY - OUR POSITION IN CHRIST	27
REVIEW LESSON 4	33
LESSON 5 FELLOWSHIP AND WATER BAPTISM	35
REVIEW LESSON 5	39
LESSON 6 THE HOLY SPIRIT	41
REVIEW LESSON 6	47
LESSON 7 SHARING YOUR FAITH	49
REVIEW LESSON 7	53
LESSON 8 HEALING and the Laying on of Hands	55
REVIEW LESSON 8	63
LESSON 9 A NEW LIFESTYLE	65
REVIEW LESSON 9	71

LESSON 10 THE CHURCH	73
REVIEW LESSON 10	77
What Christian leaders around the world are saying about "The Foundations."	79
Endorsement captions	92

FORWARD

My brother, Howard Sands has made a mark in my life and among the pastors of Maranatha Ministry. He has opened his heart in Making your Mark and made me realise how much I need to work in my leadership to Disciple and to give Foundation truth to be a leader among the leaders. Reading the book led me to pray like Dawson Trotman, 'Oh Lord, help me to build men, strong, holy, prepared men to go to the four corners of the world who will make their mark in the lives of people'.

Rev Dr Charles Finny Joseph,

President, Maranatha Ministry, Chennai, India.

General Secretary, Synod of Pentecost Churches.

INTRODUCTION

This set of teaching notes on the foundations of the Christian life came to be written because my wife Joy and I had the privilege of leading people to Christ and pastoring a beautiful congregation of people in the church we pioneered at Canberra New Life Centre, Canberra, A.C.T., Australia.

When people come to know Christ as their Lord and Saviour they need instruction in the Word of God to help them become established in the Christian life. We saw a need in the area of foundational Christian teaching material, much of which did not include all the things that we thought were relevant for a new believer. So, this short course of foundational material came to be written to encourage those new believers, and many others that came into our congregation without ever having had these foundational truths taught and explained.

To you people I thank you for allowing us to help you and to all the other members of the congregation, I thank you for your continual support of us and those new believers.

THE FOUNDATIONS

1 Corinthians 3:11 'For no one can lay any foundation other than the one already laid, which is Jesus Christ'.

2 Timothy 3:16 'All Scripture is God-breathed and is useful for teaching, rebuking, correcting and training in righteousness.'

1 Peter 2:2 'Like newborn babies, crave pure spiritual milk, so that by it you may grow up in your salvation.'

This series of studies is based on the Bible as God's infallible word to us, by which we may live our lives. We will consider it as the maker's instruction manual, our Father knows what is needful for us and He has put it in His word. Now it is up to us to discover it, know it and apply it to our lives, then we will be able to live like He intended for us to live.

LESSON 1 COMING TO CHRIST

The terms:-

Coming to Christ,	Becoming a child of God,
Being saved,	Asking Christ into your life,
Being born again,	Taking Jesus as your Lord and Saviour,

all refer to the experience of meeting God in a personal way. Whilst being born again happens in a moment of time when we are translated out of the Kingdom of darkness (Satan's Kingdom) into the Kingdom of His Son (God's Kingdom); Colossians 1:13 there is all the same a process that takes place. We will briefly look at that process.

repentance--- faith--- salvation--- forgiveness--- assurance---

REPENTANCE

When Peter preached his first sermon on the day of Pentecost and told the people how God had made Jesus, whom they crucified, both

Lord and Christ and the people were "cut to the heart" (Acts 2:37) they asked, "What must we do". Peter replied, "Repent, be baptised and you will receive the Holy Spirit."

What is Repentance?

To repent means to "about face", to turn away from sin and towards God. It means to turn, not only from all the evil we have done, but also from trying to appease God with self righteous good works.

To be truly repentant is to be heartily sorry for our sins against His laws. We will want to adopt a new life style. When we reach this point, we have taken the second step. Proverbs 28:13 Repentance means leaving sin behind and going the other way. Sin means: not being up to God's standard, not living right.

FAITH (and Believing)

Everyone has faith (Romans 12:3) of some kind or another but where is it directed? All of us are believing something all the time. Not all we believe is good and right. Now you have become a Christian it is only the Word of God that should direct your believing.

The Word of God is the foundation for our believing.

We build our faith in the Word of God. Romans 10:17.

Faith is essential for us to come to God.

Hebrews 11:6

When we express the faith in our hearts with our mouth we will be saved. Romans 10:8-9.

SALVATION

The greatest message ever told is that God loved us while we were not worthy of His love, (while we despised and rejected Him), so that if we would only believe, he would forgive our sin and give us eternal life. John. 3:16

He came to give us abundant life. John. 10:10

We were all sinners. Romans 3:23

All we deserved was death and eternal separation from God. Romans 6:23

But God loved us while we were still sinners.

Romans 5:8-9

Jesus paid the price of death on our behalf.

1 Corinthians 15:3-6

Jesus is the only way we can come to God. John. 14:6

If we receive Christ, we will become a child of God. John. 1:12

This is God's gift of grace, there is nothing we can do to earn or deserve it. Ephesians 2:8-9

To receive it we need to confess with our mouth and believe in our heart and we shall be saved. Romans 10:8-10

If you ask Christ to come in He will come in and have fellowship with you. Revelation 3:20

Have you asked Him? If not, why not do it now.

FORGIVENESS

We know we have done things that offend God (anything that offends God is sin) but if we will confess it to Him and ask His forgiveness, He will wipe our slate clean. 1 John 1:9

If we want something from God, we should ask in Jesus name. John 16:24

He will remove our sins completely. Psalms 103:12

ASSURANCE

We know that if we repent and ask His forgiveness He will forgive us, He will come into our life and give us eternal life if we believe. 1 John 5:11-13

When we ask Him in, we become brand new people (2 Corinthians 5:17) and He gives us His nature (the nature of righteousness - right standing with God, able to stand in the presence of God, the devil or man without any fear, guilt or condemnation) because we have been made holy as God is holy because we have been given His nature. 2 Corinthians 5:21

We have the ability to stand in the presence of God without condemnation Romans 8:1 so therefore let us come boldly to obtain his mercy. Hebrews 4:16

CONCLUSION

Real faith in God is based on the Bible, the Word of God, and must be confessed aloud. Why not bow in prayer now and confess aloud that you trust him, and that Jesus is your Lord and Saviour? If you need victory over temptation, or healing from sickness, or deliverance from demon powers, or his peace in place of anxiety ask the Lord for it in faith and then confess your trust in him that it now is, even as you confess it. For our trust is in the word of God not the circumstances around us, they are facts, but they must change to line up with the truth of God's Word!

Here is a suggested prayer to receive Christ as your Lord.

It is not the words of this prayer that are important but rather that you pray it from your heart.

Heavenly Father I come to you in Jesus name, knowing that my life does not measure up to your standard and that I have sinned and offended you in my thoughts, words and deeds, I now come to you on the basis of what Jesus Christ did on the cross of Calvary and ask for your forgiveness, I repent, I turn away from those things that are displeasing to you and ask for your help in my life in keeping my heart and motives pure before you. I have no ability on my own to receive anything from you, but I acknowledge Jesus as my Lord and commit my life to him and thank you that you forgive me and make me a brand-new creation now in Jesus name. I receive your forgiveness and cleansing now. Amen.

Between now and the time for you to do lesson 2 complete the answers to the ten questions on lesson 1. Look up the appropriate Scriptures, make sure that your answer comes from the Word of God, not what you think it ought to be.

REVIEW LESSON 1

COMING TO CHRIST

1/ What is the foundation upon which we must build our Christian Life? 1 Corinthians 3:11

_____

_____

2/ In this world there are two kingdoms,

one is _____ Kingdom

and the other is _____ Kingdom.

3/ What does repentance mean?

_____

_____

4/ Read 2 Corinthians 7:10-11. Is God challenging you to repentance in any areas such as relationships, habits, possessions, restitution?

_____

_____

5/ Why is faith so important? Hebrews 11:6, Mark. 16:16

_____

_____

6/ As a result of faith, what is your relationship with God? John. 1:12

_____

_____

7/ In which Scripture will you find Jesus' promise of abundant life?

_____

_____

8/ What good things do we have to do to earn God's gift of grace and eternal life? Ephesians 2:8-9

_____

_____

9/ If we confess our sin to God and ask Him to forgive us, what will He do? 1 John 1:9

_____

_____

10/ When Christ comes into your life does that make you a better person or a brand-new person? 2 Corinthians 5:17

_____

_____

Write here any things you don't fully understand and want to ask your pastor or leader.

_____

_____

LESSON 2 THE WORD OF GOD

WHAT IS THE BIBLE?

The Bible is God's Word to man - written by many different authors but all moved and inspired by the same great Holy Spirit.

2 Timothy 3:16-17 All scripture is God breathed...

God's Written Word –

Originally man was to live by "God's Will" just by being obedient to his conscience.

This failed in the Garden of Eden and God caused "His will" to be written down.

He chose a specific people - the Israelites - to receive and preserve His written will.

"Moses received living words to give to us" (Acts 7:38) starting with the Law on Mt Sinai.

The written word of God was given to about 40 people over a period of about 1500 years from approx. 1400 BC to 97AD.

The Israelites jealously preserved these writings intact although they often failed to live by them.

The Bible is not one book but a collection of 66 books:

Old Testament - 39 books covering the topics of:

Law, History, Poetry, Major and Minor Prophets.

New Testament - 27 books covering the topics of:

Biography, History, Christian Church Letters, Apocalyptic Revelation.

Testament = will, God's will for you, there are 30,000 promises there for you to inherit.

As a child comes into this life we care for it and nourish it, first with milk, then with soft foods, then more substantial foods. So also, must the newly born-again Christian be nourished to maturity.

1 Peter 2:2 pure spiritual milk

John. 6:32-35 Jesus is our bread

1 Corinthians 3:1-3 we need to mature before we eat meat

Jesus said that we are to live by every word of God in Matthew 4:4

By having the Scriptures in our heart, we can know the way God wants us to live and His promises for us to live victoriously in every aspect of life. Not having a regular intake of this spiritual food will stunt our spiritual life.

Psalms 119:9 How can a young man keep his way pure? By living according to your word.

Psalms 119.11 I have hidden your word in my heart that I might not sin against you.

The Bible is the primary source available through which God reveals himself to man, and thus is foundational to Christianity. It is a historical and therefore unchangeable record, it is a commentary on God's actions, and contains God's actual spoken words to man.

The Bible must be respected and evaluated in this light and cannot be easily dismissed.

Consider some of the things the Word of God will do for you.

1. It produces life. John 6:63
   God's word is creative Hebrews 11:3 Just as God's word brought order and light out of chaos and darkness; His word will produce the life of Christ in your heart.
2. It Uncovers Sin. Hebrews 4:12
   It is a powerful word, and it alone can expose us for what we really are. As we allow the Word of God to work in our lives, like a surgeon's scalpel, the cutting produces a healing 2 Timothy 3:16-17
3. It Cleanses Our Lifestyle. Psalms 119:9,11
   The Word of God gives us a standard to follow, and also gives us the power to live up to that standard.
4. It Produces Growth. 1 Peter 2:2
   Newborn babes cannot survive without the nutritional value of milk. Baby Christians, similarly, need the milk of God's Word.

5. It is a Weapon in our Hands. Ephesians 6:17
   With the Word of God in our hands, we can overcome the enemy in every situation. Think about David and Goliath! (1 Samuel 17:45)
6. It Gives Us Prayer Power. John. 15:7

It is not enough to just 'go through' the Word of God - we must let the Word of God go through us!

As you allow the Word of God to make its home in your heart, your prayer life will become effective.

It is good to read God's Word every day, so He can speak to you through His Word.

You should get to know your Bible because it will help you in every situation you find yourself.

Proverbs 4:22 It is life to those who find it and health to all their flesh.

Hosea 4:6 My people are destroyed because they reject the truth.

John. 8:32 You will know the truth and the truth will set you free.

Learn to live by God's word; not your feelings - because feelings change from day to day, but God's Word never changes.

Matthew 24:35 Heaven and earth will disappear, but my words will remain for ever.

REVIEW LESSON 2

THE WORD OF GOD

1. How many books are there in the Bible?
   _____

2. Complete this sentence. God's Word is His
   _____

3. What kind of food do new Christians require?
   _____

4. How can we know God's will?
   _____

5. How long will God's word last? Matthew 24:35
   _____

6. What does God's word produce?
   _____

7. What does God's word uncover?
   _____

8. How many situations can the word of God be applied to, to help us overcome?
   _____

9. Where should the word of God live?
   _____

10. Why is it important to live by God's word and not our feelings?
    _____
    _____

Here is a good place to write any questions about the word of God for discussion with your pastor or group leader.

_____
_____

LESSON 3 PRAYER

When a baby is born, its immediate needs are food, warmth and air. For the reborn Christian, his food is the Word of God; he finds warmth in fellowship with other Christians, and as he prays to God it is like breathing the fresh, clean air of heaven.

Prayer is important -for the individual and for the Church. The Bible teaches a lot on prayer.

Prayer is talking with God! It is called dialogue. Two-way conversation, talking and listening.

You get to know God by spending time with Him. Just as a husband gets to know his wife better each year of marriage - so as you spend time with God you will get to know Him better and better, and your understanding of His character and His ways deepen.

His voice will become familiar to you and you will respond to Him, on a daily basis.

With Jesus Christ as your Saviour and Lord, you have the unique privilege of speaking directly with your heavenly Father through Him. God wants you to come confidently into his presence through Christ and to talk to him about everything.

Philippians 4:6 and Hebrews 4:14-16

He is intensely interested in you and your needs.

Praying is putting our lives in our words, Pray without ceasing is a lifestyle. We may consider what an earthly father will do for his children, but our heavenly Father is so much more interested in our daily lives and wellbeing, His care for us is beyond our understanding and knows no limits.

Matthew 6.25-32

When we come to God in prayer Jesus taught us to acknowledge God as Father, we can only say that when we are born again, it is then that He has become our Father. He is everything we would like our earthly father to have been.

We come to God as our response to His calling, it is His initiative that brought us home not ours, we come to a limitless God. We now belong to His family.

As we regularly come to God in prayer, it should be a part of our daily routine as well as an immediate response to need and a part of our lives in all aspects. Prayer doesn't have to be long, but it can be.

Prayer doesn't need to be religious it needs to be from the heart, we don't need to say repetitious prayers we need to express our heart to our loving heavenly Father.

However, prayer is not disrespectful, we should give reverence to His name, not in a religious kind of way but honouring Him with praise and thanks for who He is as well as what He has done generally and for us specifically.

Does my life show that I love the Lord?

As God's son, do I reflect God's love in the world around me?

Pray with Confidence 1 John. 5:14-15

Knowing that your praying is in the will of God, you can confidently expect results. To put 'if it be your will' in your prayers usually indicates a lack of knowledge and/or faith.

We know God's will by knowing His word. His word is His will.

Knowing God's will before we pray gives us the right to an answer, at all times.

In the Lord's prayer, it says, "Your will be done on earth as it is in heaven." Jesus was teaching His disciples to pray that God's will would be done on earth because God's will is always done in heaven.

Jesus was saying pray that it happens, you are the instruments of His will, we become the fulfilment of that prayer as we, who know the will of God, start to implement it in our daily lives.

When you pray, don't talk all the time, be a listener, listen for God, wait on Him, abide in Him, let His words rest in you, let them become part of you, repeat God's word back to him. When you pray the word, you know you are praying in God's will. John 15.7

Sin may block an answer sometimes, and sometimes God will delay the answer in order to prove our faith - but if our heart does not condemn us, we know that we have what we prayed.

1 John 3:20-22; James 5:16

We don't need to be continually confessing our sin and repenting, we did that when we first came to Christ and the blood of Jesus Christ God's son cleanses us from all sin. 1 John 1.7 Now as a born-again believer we have come into His family, we have been restored and translated out of darkness into light, we need to thank Him for His grace in forgiving us and strengthening us to walk in His ways.

Repentance, as we already discovered, is turning around and walking in the opposite direction, so we walk away from the things we know that displease God and thank him for His cleansing that was applied to our life when we first believed and receive that forgiveness and move on.

Salvation is not lost because we fail another time, if we sin we have an advocate with the Father.

1 John 2.1 We ask for and receive forgiveness, we admit our fault, making no excuses, nor blaming anyone else. We then rest in the Father, we are now forgiven and free to forgive others.

John 16:24 Until now you have not asked for anything in my name. Ask and you will receive, and your joy will be full.

Keys for an effective prayer life.

1. **Give it priority.**
   You are making an appointment with the King of the Universe. Don't, not show up.
2. **Set a definite time.**
   Usually first thing in the morning, there is no value putting on the armour after the battle.

3. **Find a quiet place.**

   Jesus said go to your closet, pray in secret, Jesus went away to pray.

4. **Get mentally awake.**

   Wash your face, stand up, go for a walk etc.

5. **Prepare your heart.**

   Ask God to speak to you, come expectant.

6. **Listen to God.**

   Take Bible, pen and notebook, write down your thoughts as God speaks to you.

7. **Talk to the Lord.**

Talk to Jesus as you would to anyone else.

Religious language won't get you any favours in heaven.

24 - HOWARD SANDS

REVIEW LESSON 3

PRAYER

1. On the basis of which scripture can we come boldly and confidently into God's presence and pray to Him?
   _____

2. Explain based on Matthew 6.25-32, how interested God is in your daily life.
   _____

3. How do we know God's will?
   _____

4. What are some reasons we may not receive an answer from God to our prayer?
   _____

5. What can we do about these reasons for not receiving?
   _____

6. How do we best get to know God?
   _____

7. In whose name should we pray? John. 16:24
   _____

8. Where must God's Word be for answered prayer? John. 15:7

9. How do we get the peace of God? Philippians 4:6-7

10. What is the right reaction to have towards difficult circumstances? Philippians 4:6-7

What would you like to ask your pastor or leader this week about what you have been studying? Make a note of it here.

LESSON 4 VICTORY - OUR POSITION IN CHRIST

2 Corinthians 5:17 "Therefore, if anyone is in Christ, he is a new creation; the old has gone, the new has come!"

Since we made a decision to ask Christ into our life we are no longer the same as we used to be. The Bible tells us in this passage that if any person is in Christ, (we are in the Body of Christ, that is the church; when He is in us, and He came to be in us when we asked Him to forgive us and come into our life; therefore this passage is talking to all born again believers) YOU ARE A NEW CREATION, the old has gone and a new you has come.

Colossians 1:13 The old you was in the Kingdom of darkness but the new you has been brought out of that Kingdom which has Satan as its king and brought into the Kingdom of His Son which has Jesus as its king.

Romans 12:2 We need to take a hold with our mind, of the things that have happened to us by renewing our mind to think about us like God thinks about us.

Transformed means: - to transform, to change from one state to another totally different state, in the way that an earth-bound caterpillar turns into a beautiful butterfly that can flit from flower to flower without being bound to the earth.

Every believer is by faith identified with Christ in His death, resurrection and ascension to the throne of God. Therefore, we accept our identification with Him and we share in His victory.

Ephesians 2.4-6

You have been given fullness in Christ, everything Christ has he has given you when you were placed in Him at the time of your new birth. Colossians 2.10. He is the head over every power and authority and He has put His name, His authority, His power in you, to exercise that power and authority in the spiritual realms on His behalf.

God's Spirit now dwells in you as a result of the new birth, it is the practical result of regeneration and is the reason for the victory that we can now exercise in the world.

Colossians 1.27 tells us what this mystery of the new birth is, it is what the old testament saints and prophets longed to see and understand even though only a few of them caught a glimpse of it. It is that Christ is in you and that is the hope that we have of the glory of God at work in our lives.

The reason and strength of our victory over circumstances of life is that Christ is in us by His Spirit, He is greater than he who is in the world, (that is the devil). I John 4.4. We need to use this authority and position of victory that we have over the devil and start to command him to leave our lives, our circumstances, our finances, our families, our health etc. We need to speak about the victorious position we have in Christ and command the blessings that God has ordained for us to be allowed to freely flow in our lives.

Here are some of the things God says about you.

Say them out loud now as though they belong to you, because they do.

Colossians 2:9-10 *For in Christ all the fullness of the Deity lives in bodily form, and you have been given fullness in Christ, who is the head over every power and authority.*

I HAVE EVERYTHING because I have Christ, and I am filled with God through my union with Christ.

Romans 8:2 *...because through Christ Jesus the law of the Spirit of life set me free from the law of sin and death.*

I AM set free from the law of sin and death.

2 Corinthians 5:21 *God made him who had no sin to be sin for us, so that in him we might become the righteousness of God.*

I HAVE a righteous nature.

Philippians 3:9 *and be found in him, not having a righteousness of my own that comes from the law, but that which is through faith in Christ —the righteousness that comes from God and is by faith.*

I POSSESS the righteousness which is of God.

Righteousness means: - the ability to stand in the presence of God or man without the sense of fear, condemnation or guilt.

Ephesians 1:3 *Praise be to the God and Father of our Lord Jesus Christ, who has blessed us in the heavenly realms with every spiritual blessing in Christ.*

I HAVE ALL spiritual blessings

2 Corinthians 9:8 *And God is able to make all grace abound to you, so that in all things, at all times, having all that you need, you will abound in every good work.*

God is able to make ALL grace (every favour and earthly blessing) come to ME in abundance

2 Peter 1:3 *His divine power has given us everything we need for life and godliness through our knowledge of him who called us by his own glory and goodness.*

His Divine power has given to me ALL things that pertain to life and godliness.

Romans 8:37 *No, in all these things we are more than conquerors through him who loved us.*

I am more than a conqueror through Him (Jesus) that loves me.

1 Corinthians 6:19 *Do you not know that your body is a temple of the Holy Spirit, who is in you, whom you have received from God? You are not your own;*

My body is the temple of the Holy Spirit.

1 Peter 2:24 *He himself bore our sins in his body on the tree, so that we might die to sins and live for righteousness; by his wounds you have been healed.*

By His stripes I WAS healed.

Philippians 4:13 *I can do everything through him who gives me strength.*

I CAN do all things through Christ who strengthens me.

Philippians 4:19 *And my God will meet all your needs according to his glorious riches in Christ Jesus.*

My God supplies ALL my needs according to his riches in glory by Christ Jesus.

Ephesians 2:6 *And God raised us up with Christ and seated us with him in the heavenly realms in Christ Jesus,*

He Has seated me together with Christ in heavenly places.

Ephesians 1:20-23 *which he exerted in Christ when he raised him from the dead and seated him at his right hand in the heavenly realms, 21 far above all rule and authority, power and dominion, and every title that can be given, not only in the present age but also in the one to come. 22 And God placed all things under his feet and appointed him to be head over everything for the church, 23 which is his body, the fullness of him who fills everything in every way.*

I am in the body, Christ is the head, all things are under his feet and therefore under my feet too.

Colossians 2:9-10 *For in Christ all the fullness of the Deity lives in bodily form, 10 and you have been given fullness in Christ, who is the head over every power and authority.*

I AM COMPLETE in Christ

1 Corinthians 15:57 *But thanks be to God! He gives us the victory through our Lord Jesus Christ.*

I LIVE IN THE VICTORY that Christ has given to me.

John 14:13-14 *And I will do whatever you ask in my name, so that the Son may bring glory to the Father. 14 You may ask me for anything in my name, and I will do it.*

Therefore, WHATEVER I ASK the Father in Jesus name He will do it.

These are some of the things God says about you; these are the same things you should say about you, even when circumstances do not agree.

The circumstances are fact but God's word is truth.

Facts will change but the truth never changes.

Therefore, we can change the facts by applying the truth.

Learn to say about you what God's word says about you and you will learn to live in the victory of what Christ has won for you.

REVIEW LESSON 4

VICTORY - OUR POSITION IN CHRIST

1. 2 Corinthians 5:17 Now you are in Christ, what are you?
   _____

2. Romans 12:2 What do we need to do to our mind?
   _____

3. Romans 8:2 What has the law of the Spirit of life in Jesus Christ made you free from?
   _____

4. 2 Corinthians 5:21 What kind of a nature does every born-again Christian have?
   _____

5. What does righteous mean?
   _____

6. How many of your needs will God meet?
   _____

7. When did you receive healing for your body? 2 Peter 2:24
   _____

8. How many things can you do because God strengthens you? Philippians 4:13

   _____

9. What areas are there in your life where you need to trust God, and rely on His Word?

   _____
   _____

10. In order for God to do anything for us what must we do? John 14:13-14

    _____
    _____

Now do what you should do about the areas in question 9.

LESSON 5 FELLOWSHIP AND WATER BAPTISM

PURPOSE OF FELLOWSHIP

Welcome to God's family. When you accepted Jesus Christ as your one and only Lord in your life you became a part of God's family.

John 1:12 You became a child of God.

Everyone needs a family - now you are a part of the biggest family in the world - the church of the Lord Jesus Christ - and you have brothers and sisters all over the world.

Psalms 68:6 He sets the solitary in families.

It is important for your growth as a Christian to spend time in fellowship with your brothers and sisters so that -

- you can be taught in the word of God;

- you can receive encouragement and help from other Christians;

- you can help and encourage others.

You become like the people you hang around with, someone once said, "If you hang around with a dog long enough you'll end up getting fleas."

It is important to fellowship mostly, with those that you can learn from, people who will encourage your faith and strengthen you, so that when you do meet with non-Christian people, you have something built into you that you can give them.

Get to as many church meetings as you can, the word of God and the presence of God will work a change in your life.

Hebrews 10:25 What do you think this means?

Find people of like mind and vision and have fellowship with them.

Galatians 6:10 The New Testament tells us the church is a household.

Hebrews 3:6 Jesus is the head of the house.

Galatians 4:7 You are not a servant but a son in this household.

Servants are replaceable;

Visitors are temporary, (or ought to be);

Boarders are free to come and go as they please;

but as a Son, you are an important part of the household - an heir.

Make the church your family and make it your habit to participate in it regularly as Jesus did.

Luke 4:16

Our fellowship with God is affected by our fellowship with one another, but even if there are problems there, God wants us to put aside those things that separate us and walk together in fellowship with one another. 1 John 1.7

WATER BAPTISM

What is the next step after believing the gospel?

Mark 16:15-16

If you have been christened or baptised as a baby or prior to yielding your life to Christ that would not suffice to meet the command of Christ to be baptised as we are told that repentance must precede baptism. It is not possible for a baby or a very young child to repent as they cannot understand the concept of what is involved. Acts 2:38, 8:12 and 37 only believers were baptised.

The Scriptures prove that baptism is by immersion fully into the water, Phillip and the eunuch Acts 8:38 "led him into the water" and "came up out of the water."

How soon after conversion should baptism take place?

No delay. Acts 8:36-38, 22:16, 10:47-48, 16:33

Is baptism optional?

The commands of Christ cannot be considered as optional. A command is to be complied with.

Matthew 28:19-20

Willingness to keep his commands is proof of our love. John. 14:15, 21, 23

Following Christ's example.

Matthew 3:13-15, 1 Peter 2:21

What is the purpose of baptism?

It shows our obedience to His command.

Matt 28:19, Mark 16.16

It is an open confession of our faith and the answer of a good conscience towards God.

1 Peter 3:21

It is symbolic of the washing away of our sins Acts 22:16 which is only accomplished by the blood of Jesus Christ. Revelation 1:5

What do we learn from baptism?

Baptism is an illustration of death, Romans 6:3-8, Christ endured the actual baptism of death for us. Symbolically in our baptism we die with Christ and like as Jesus was raised from the dead, so we also walk in a new life. Galatians 2:20

REVIEW LESSON 5

FELLOWSHIP AND WATER BAPTISM

1. When did you become a child of God? John. 1:12
   _____

2. What do you learn about fellowship from Hebrews 10:24-25?
   _____
   _____

3. What is the basis of our fellowship? Galatians 3:28
   _____

4. How does our relationship with God affect our fellowship with one another? 1 John 1:7
   _____
   _____

5. What do you learn about fellowship from 1 Corinthians 1:10?
   _____

6. Why is it important to be baptised? 1 Peter 3:21
   _____

7. What was the attitude of the early apostles to water baptism?
   _____

8. Who should be baptised?
   _____

9. What must precede baptism?
   _____

10. Baptism is an illustration of what? Romans 6:3-8
    _____

What would you like to ask your pastor or leader this week about what you have been studying? Make a note of it here.

LESSON 6 THE HOLY SPIRIT

1 John 5:7 The Holy Spirit is God, called the third person of the Godhead (not because He is third in position, ranking or power; but because He has the third ministry on the earth) He is equal to God because He is God. His purpose is to bear witness to Christ, to bring sons to birth and equip them for the Christian life.

1 Corinthians 12:13 When we are born again (accept Christ, come into God's family), it is a work of the Holy Spirit, He is not a stranger to you for you have already met Him.

God the Father is already seated in heaven. Jesus the Son sat down at God's right hand after he was raised from the dead. Ephesians 1:20, Hebrews 1:3, 1 Peter 3:22

The Holy Spirit is the active power of God at work in the earth today. His job is to reveal God's Word to you and confirm God's Word by demonstrating God's power.

He is the one who supernaturally empowers us so that we can live "not by might, nor by power but by my Spirit says the Lord." Zechariah 4:6

John the Baptist said Jesus would baptise us in the Holy Spirit. Matthew 3:11

Jesus Himself was baptised with the Holy Spirit for His earthly ministry. Luke. 3:21-22

Jesus spoke about the Holy Spirit, that He would come after Jesus death. John. 15:26

Jesus said we should receive the Holy Spirit by asking the Father for Him. Luke. 11:13

Jesus said the Baptism in the Holy Spirit was like being filled with a river. John. 7:37-39

After His death, but before His ascension into heaven, Jesus told the disciples to wait in Jerusalem for the Holy Spirit to come upon them and they would be endued with power. Luke. 24:49, Acts 1:8

Jesus said that believers would speak with new tongues. Mark. 16:17

The Holy Spirit who had been **with** the disciples before Pentecost (John. 14:16-17) was later powerfully **in** them as Jesus baptised about 120 of them in the Holy Spirit according to His promise. Acts 2:4

Receiving the baptism in the Holy Spirit is accompanied by a sign (a new sign for a new dispensation), speaking in other tongues. This is speaking in a language that you have never learned. It is basically a prayer language that the Holy Spirit uses to pray through you when you are yielded to Him. He prays through you to God the Father and knows exactly what to pray, even though you may not know how or what. 1 Corinthians 14:2, Romans 8:26-27

The example of Jesus and the disciples was followed by the early church, they received the baptism in the Holy Spirit and taught that all believers should also receive the same.

Acts 2:38, 8:14-20, 9:17, 10:44-48, 11:15-17, 19:6-7, Ephesians 1:13

From the moment of the new birth every Christian has available to them all that Christ has, including the gift of the Holy Spirit. Ephesians 1:3, Colossians 2:10

We receive the promise of the Holy Spirit just the same way as we received Jesus into our life, BY ASKING IN FAITH. Galatians 3:2, 14

The book of Acts, supported by the gospels (biographies of Jesus) and epistles (letters of the early apostles), shows that the supernatural ability to speak in tongues is the normal immediate accompaniment of the baptism in the Holy Spirit. More than 20 years after the Holy Spirit was first poured out speaking in tongues was still taken as the initial evidence that believers had received the Holy Spirit, a lack of speaking in tongues was evidence they had not yet been filled with the Holy Spirit. Acts 19:1-6

Some other gifts which may also accompany the baptism in the Holy Spirit, which we should eagerly seek include those in 1 Corinthians 12:8-10: word of wisdom, word of knowledge, discerning of spirits, faith, healings, miracles, prophecy, tongues, interpretation of tongues.

Some of the reasons that God has provided this unique supernatural experience are that: -

- you may be built up in the spirit,
  1 Corinthians 14:4, 14-15, Jude 20
- you may pray and intercede in the Spirit,
  Ephesians 6:18, Romans 8:26
- you may worship God in the spirit,
  John. 4:23-24.
- so that you may be witnesses of Jesus in all the world. Acts 1:8.

If you have not yet received the baptism in the Holy Spirit, with the initial evidence of speaking in other tongues, why not ask God for it now.

Ask someone who has received the baptism in the Holy Spirit to pray with you in the New Testament pattern, laying their hands on you and ask God to give you His Holy Spirit, expect to receive immediately.

Here is a suggested prayer to receive the baptism in the Holy Spirit

It is not the words of this prayer that are important but rather that you pray it from your heart.

Father, I now want to go one step further. I now want to receive the Baptism of your Holy Spirit, the release of your Holy Spirit to flow over me and fill me to overflowing in my inner most being.

Father, in the name of Your Son Jesus Christ, I thank you that I now receive the Holy Spirit in all His fullness, I receive every gift that you have for me and will by faith walk in them and use them for your glory as you reveal yourself in and to me.

Thank you, Father.

Thank you, Jesus.

REVIEW LESSON 6

THE HOLY SPIRIT

1. When are we baptised into the body of Christ? 1 Corinthians 12:13

   _____

2. Who baptises us in the Holy Spirit?

   _____

3. Do the events at 1 and 2 above always happen at the same time?

   _____

4. What happened to Jesus immediately after he was water baptised?

   _____

5. Why did Jesus tell the disciples to wait in Jerusalem? Luke 24:49

   _____

6. Why do all Christians need the baptism in the Holy Spirit?

   _____

   _____

7. How do we receive the Holy Spirit? Luke. 11:13

   _____
   _____

8. What is the normal initial evidence of having received the baptism in the Holy Spirit?

   _____

9. Have you received the baptism in the Holy Spirit?

   _____

   If not pray now and ask God for this gift right now.
   If yes, who can you pray for to receive the Holy Spirit?

   _____

10. What is the ongoing purpose of speaking in other tongues?

    _____
    _____

LESSON 7 SHARING YOUR FAITH

Jesus last command to His disciples was to go and tell the world about Him and what He had taught them during His ministry time with them.

Mark 16:15 He said to them, Go into all the world and preach the good news to all creation.

Matthew 28:19-20 Therefore go and make disciples of all nations, baptizing them in the name of the Father and of the Son and of the Holy Spirit, and teaching them to obey everything I have commanded you. And surely, I am with you always, to the very end of the age.

Acts 1:8 But you will receive power when the Holy Spirit comes on you; and you will be my witnesses in Jerusalem, and in all Judea and Samaria, and to the ends of the earth.

Jesus had prepared His disciples during three years of ministry and had sent them out to share the good news on several occasions (Luke 10:1-9) as a training for the ministry to which He had called them. He instructed them just prior to His death to wait in Jerusalem for the gift of the Holy Spirit before going out. Acts 1.4

It is apparent that Jesus had prepared His disciples to be active sharers of the good news that He had delivered to them and that this same instruction is passed down to us who believe in these days. It is also clear that Jesus wanted His disciples to be empowered with the Holy Spirit for this task and not to do it in their own strength.

After Peter and the disciples received the baptism of the Holy Spirit on the Day of Pentecost, Peter's first reaction to the questioning of those that saw and heard these events was to share the gospel message about Jesus being crucified and that they should repent for the forgiveness of their sins, be baptised and they too would receive this gift of the Holy Spirit. Acts 2:14-40

Jesus had prepared His disciples by teaching, training and then infilling them with the Holy Spirit as a fulfilment of His promise, for the purpose of having His disciples to be ready at all occasions to deliver the message that he had delivered to them.

Timothy 4:2 Preach the Word; be prepared in season and out of season;...

Paul and the early disciples were always sharing the gospel message.

Acts 5:42 Day after day, in the temple courts and from house to house, they never stopped teaching and proclaiming the good news that Jesus is the Christ.

Acts 20:21 I have declared to both Jews and Greeks that they must turn to God in repentance and have faith in our Lord Jesus.

Paul provides us some teaching on the need to preach the gospel.

Romans 10:14-15 How, then, can they call on the one they have not believed in? And how can they believe in the one of whom they have not heard? And how can they hear without someone preaching to them? And how can they preach unless they are sent? As it is written, "How beautiful are the feet of those who bring good news!"

Paul is suggesting here that the gospel message must be delivered to those that have never heard it, and that this is the only way in which those that have never heard the gospel will come to believe in and call upon Jesus the Saviour.

In addition, he quotes from the Old Testament prophet Isaiah and tells us that those who share the good news of Jesus Christ are people having beautiful feet. This is a commendation on those that bring the message of Christ (the good news).

Isaiah 52:7 How beautiful on the mountains are the feet of those who bring good news, who proclaim peace, who bring good tidings, who proclaim salvation, who say to Zion, "Your God reigns!"

Paul felt so strongly about the need to share the good news that he felt an inner compulsion to preach the gospel freely to all. This was not a religious duty but an inner compulsion, such was the difference that the gospel had made to him that it became the motivating force of his life.

1 Corinthians 9:16 Yet when I preach the gospel, I cannot boast, for I am compelled to preach. Woe to me if I do not preach the gospel!

When we really encounter Christ and are saved He makes a difference in our life, but this difference is not for us alone. You are not saved only so that you can enjoy the benefits of belonging to Christ, but that you may be a witness to others also.

This week think about those that you know (family, friends, work mates, neighbours) and plan to share something of your faith in Christ with them. It may be in one or more ways and may include but not necessarily be limited to, Sharing how you came to receive Christ as your Lord; Sharing how we all have the need of a saviour to save us from the penalty of sin; Sharing how Christ has changed your outlook on life; Sharing an answer to prayer that you have received; Sharing how someone you know or have recently met through other Christians has received an answer to prayer.

Make a decision to talk to someone about Christ in some aspect every day of your life.

Remember to ask the people you talk to if they have received Christ in their life, if not ask them if they would like to and if they say they would, you lead them in a simple prayer of receiving Christ, explaining to them the things you are learning in this booklet.

Ask God each morning in prayer for His Holy Spirit to flow through you that day and give you encounters with people where you can share your faith.

Proverbs 28:1 …the righteous are bold as a lion.

Talk about this next week with your leader, talk about the experiences you have had during the week.

REVIEW LESSON 7

SHARING YOUR FAITH

1. What was Jesus last command to His disciples?
   _____
   _____

2. What did Jesus tell the disciples to teach the new believers to obey?
   _____
   _____

3. Acts 1:8 Where do you think this means you should be a witness?
   _____

4. What was Peter's first reaction to the questioning of those that saw and heard the events of the Holy Spirit being poured out on them?
   _____

5. Acts 5:42 What did they never stop doing?
   _____

6. Acts 20:21 What did Paul declare to both Jews and Greeks?
   _____

7. Isaiah and Paul in Romans tell us, those that share the good news of Christ are people having ....
   _____

8. What is the only way in which those that have never heard the gospel will come to believe in and call upon the Saviour?
   _____

9. Who did you talk to about Christ this week and what was the basis of your conversation?
   _____

10. Did you ask someone if they would receive Christ this week?
    _____

Share the outcome.
_____
_____

LESSON 8 HEALING and the Laying on of Hands

The gospels (Matthew, Mark, Luke & John) and the book of Acts have many accounts of both Jesus and the disciples healing the sick, with a word, a prayer, a touch etc. Part of Jesus last command was for the disciples to …place their hands on sick people, and they will get well. Mark 16.18b

There is a great need for healing today and much of the church has forgotten how to use this gift given by Jesus.

What won't get you healing is; Wishing, Wanting, Hoping or Waiting.

You need to know what God says about it and act on it.

What is needed for healing?

KNOW GODS WILL

Many believe God is able to heal but are not as confident when it comes to knowing if He WILL heal. Luke 5.11-12 While Jesus was in one of the towns, a man came along who was covered with leprosy. When he saw Jesus, he fell with his face to the ground and begged him, "Lord, if you are willing, you can make me clean." Jesus reached out his hand and touched the man. "I am willing," he said. "Be clean!" And immediately the leprosy left him.

Jesus left us in no doubt that He is willing.

Don't pray asking God to do something 'if it be your will' -Know what His will is, know what the word says, then pray according to His will.

The word says He is able.

The word says He is willing.

So, we can pray from a position of knowledge with faith.

We also know that he has given the authority over sickness and disease to the believers, the disciples were commanded to lay hands on the sick and heal them.

AUTHORITY

Know that Jesus has all authority.

"...his incomparably great power for us who believe. That power is the same as the mighty strength

20 he exerted when he raised Christ from the dead and seated him at his right hand in the heavenly realms,

21 far above all rule and authority, power and dominion, and every name that is invoked, not only in the present age but also in the one to come.

22 And God placed all things under his feet and appointed him to be head over everything for the church,

23 which is His body, the fullness of Him who fills all in all.

Ephesians 1.19-23 NIV

Transferred authority.

In Luke 9.1 Jesus gave the disciples power and authority to drive out all demons and to cure diseases.

You have His authority.

He made you complete in Him when you were born again. Christ, who is the fullness of God, is in you; Christ's authority is in you.

"And you are complete in him, who is the head of all principality and power."

Colossians 2.10 King James 2000 Bible

All authority is given to you, Go you therefore -

Then Jesus came to them and said, "All authority in heaven and on earth has been given to me. 19 Therefore go and make disciples of all nations, Matthew 28.18-19

Although Satan has deceived and afflicted many, his authority is subject to you in Jesus name. Satan's purpose is steal, kill and destroy. John 10.10

Jesus said, I have given you authority over all the power of the enemy. Luke 10.19

Jesus promised to give you, "Anything you ask in my name." John 16.23

"'If you can?" said Jesus. "Everything is possible for him who believes." Mark 9.23

DESIRE

There is a requirement that you should desire what you pray for, you must want it, hope for it. You must believe that you will receive.

Mark 11.22-24 KJV "Therefore I say to you, What things soever you desire, when you pray, believe that you receive them, and you shall have them."

EXPECTATION - your request must be in an environment of faith.

Mark 16.17 NIV And these signs will accompany those who believe: In my name they will drive out demons; they will speak in new tongues; they will pick up snakes with their hands; and when they drink deadly poison, it will not hurt them at all; they will place their hands on sick people, and they will get well."

This is a promise to those who believe.

When we speak healing in words of command to the sickness or condition, knowing it is God's will to heal, not only do we need to desire it but also fully expect that it will materialise as we speak.

PRESENCE

Luke 5.17 One day Jesus was teaching, and Pharisees and teachers of the law were sitting there. They had come from every village of Galilee and from Judea and Jerusalem. And the **power of the Lord was with Jesus to heal the sick.**

18 Some men came carrying a paralyzed man on a mat and tried to take him into the house to lay him before Jesus.

19 When they could not find a way to do this because of the crowd, they went up on the roof and lowered him on his mat through the tiles into the middle of the crowd, right in front of Jesus.

Why was it recorded that the power of the Lord was present to heal? Could it have had something to do with the faith being expressed by all those who had come from every village, expecting miracles.

Active faith brings His presence and power.

We know that where there is unbelief it limits the power of God.

"And because of their unbelief, he couldn't do any miracles among them except to place his hands on a few sick people and heal them." Mark 6.5 New Living Translation

CONFESSION

Your confession is what you are saying.

What you receive, whether it be for yourself or someone else, is determined by what you say, not what you pray. You say what you believe.

Mark 11.22-24 "Have faith in God," Jesus answered.

23 "Truly I tell you, if anyone says to this mountain, 'Go, throw yourself into the sea,' and does not doubt in their heart but believes that what they say will happen, it will be done for them.

24 Therefore I tell you, whatever you ask for in prayer, believe that you have received it, and it will be yours."

RECEIVING

Prayer for healing is not necessary to have immediate vicinity.

"The centurion replied, "Lord, I do not deserve to have you come under my roof. But just say the word, and my servant will be healed." Matthew 8.8

Jesus speaking the word brought healing to this servant some distance away.

ACTION

When we are wanting to receive, our faith must be converted into action. God spoke to the prophet Elijah "Go at once to Zarephath in the region of Sidon and stay there. I have directed a widow there to supply you with food."

1 Kings 17.9

HE ACTED – The woman didn't know she was to feed him and even said that she could not, yet she ended up doing so, as the miraculous provision of God supplied both her needs and the prophets. Elijah took action on God's word, the woman also took action on the words of the prophet to receive her miracle.

One day ten lepers met Jesus and called out in faith to Him, "Jesus, Master, have pity on us!" Jesus told the lepers to do something, their action before seeing any result (faith), caused their healing to come. "When he saw them, he said, "Go, show yourselves to the priests." And as they went, they were cleansed.

Luke 17.14

They were not healed standing there, Jesus commanded them to take action, "Go, show yourselves to the priests." And as they went, they were cleansed.

We can simplify the healing process into a small acrostic to help you remember.

FAPAM (Faith, Authority, Presence, Action, Miracles)

Laying on of hands

You will notice that Jesus and the disciples as recorded in the gospel and in Acts sometimes laid their hands on people and sometimes they did not, and people were healed both ways. Although we are told to lay hands on the sick in Jesus great commission, evidence shows us that both ways were effective for healing.

The laying on of hands is used in other circumstances other than healing.

Baptism in the Holy Spirit Acts 8.17-18

Ordaining people for a task. (elders and leaders)

Acts 13.1-3

Bestowing of spiritual gifts 1 Timothy 4.14, 2 Timothy 1.6

Blessing Mark 10.16

God uses those already prepared and anointed for a task or with a certain experience to impart that to others through the laying on of hands.

REVIEW LESSON 8

HEALING And the laying on of hands

1. How did Jesus respond to the leper in Luke 5.13
   _____

2. God placed _____ things under his _____ and appointed him to be the _____ over everything to the church. Ephesians 1.22

3. Jesus gave the disciples power to do two things in Luke 9.1
   a/_____
   b/_____

4. When were the lepers cleansed? Luke 17.14
   _____

5. What are Satan's purposes?
   _____,
   _____,
   _____

6. Jesus gave you authority over _____ the _____ of the _____ Luke 10.19

7. What is one way a spiritual gift may be bestowed on someone?
   _____

8. "Therefore, I tell you, whatever you ask for in prayer, _____ that you have _____ it, and it shall be yours." Mark 11.24

9. Is the laying on of hands necessary to bring healing?
   _____

10. Who did Jesus say would do this:
    _____

In my name they will drive out demons; they will speak in new tongues; 18 they will pick up snakes with their hands; and when they drink deadly poison, it will not hurt them at all; they will place their hands on sick people, and they will get well."

Mark 16.17/18

LESSON 9 A NEW LIFESTYLE

God has given us many privileges, but we also have certain responsibilities. The Bible tells us what God expects of us. Our response should be to obey and to thank Him for all He has done for us.

Most of the promises God makes to us in the Bible concerning our Christian growth are conditional upon our obedience to His will. Who will you live your life for? What has first place in your thoughts and plans? Jesus often challenged his disciples to consider their commitment to Him and His Kingdom. Matthew 6:33 Seek first His Kingdom and His righteousness, and all these things will be given to you as well.

Accepting Jesus Christ is the beginning of a continual walk of submission to His Lordship. The purpose of submission to God is not to just deal with sin but our submission to His way enables Him to mould us into vessels of honour. Jesus is our example of a life totally submitted to do the will of God.

Philippians 2:5-8 Those who follow his example are given many promises in the word of God.

Psalms 37:11, Psalms 149:4, Matthew 5:1-12 God wants you to be separated from your old lifestyle and be a part of the new lifestyle.

Ephesians 4:22-5:5, 2 Corinthians 6:17

However, he does not expect you to do it in your own strength but by the strength that He provides when we trust Him. Philippians 4:13

SEEDTIME AND HARVEST

The harvest principle is found right through God's Word. Simply it is; 'What you sow is what you get'. Whatever you sow; attitudes, words, finance, thoughts, deeds, that is what you will reap.

Luke 6:38, 2 Corinthians 9:6

LOVE

John 13:34-35 A new commandment I give you: Love one another as I have loved you, so, you must love one another. All men will know that you are my disciples if you love one another.

God is love and the source of love, He is the perfect example of love. His love is sacrificial. God's love is unconditional. It is not dependent on our worthiness to receive for no one can do anything to make himself worthy of God's love - yet He loves everyone. Dear friends, since God so loved us, we also ought to love one another. 1 John 4:11

In the Family

Without submission, the family unit cannot operate effectively. Each member of the family needs to submit to each other, Ephesians 5:21 says, Submitting yourselves one to another in the fear of God.

Ephesians 5:22-33 Wives: Wives are to submit to the headship of their husbands, not forced or blind obedience but voluntary submission. As she does this she reaps the benefit of his headship - liberation, nourishment, growth, built up; she is raised up by him and set free. Without voluntary submission on her part the word is useless. Submission cannot be demanded. The Father did not demand it of the Son.

It is a voluntary submission which wives are exhorted to make because it is fitting and proper; it is right in the sight of God. Paul follows with a word to husbands.

Husbands: The husband is the head of the wife and submitted to God. He submits to God by laying down his life for his wife as Christ laid down His life for the church.

Children: Colossians 3:20, Ephesians 6:1-3 As children obey their parents, they learn how to relate to God as Father, and begin to understand obedience to the Lord

In the Church

Hebrews 13:17 God has appointed ministers in the church to perfect His people. Those in a position of spiritual authority have a responsibility for our spiritual development and wellbeing, it is up to us to accept that authority. If we work with the authorities God has put over us we free His hand to accomplish His purpose in our lives, if we resist it we short circuit the effectiveness of what God wants to achieve in our lives.

In our Possessions

When you have a ham and eggs breakfast, both the pig and the hen give something. The hen makes an offering, but the pig makes a total sacrifice!

We can only become what God has intended for us when we are willing to totally lay down our agenda and be completely submissive to him in all areas of our life including our finance and possessions. In an offering we give a small portion of what we have and retain control over the rest, but God calls us to give a total sacrifice, it is all His, it is all for His use and He will allow us to use some of it for our needs. It's not our money, it is His money.

They are not our possessions, they are His possessions, we are the keepers of them on His behalf until He requires them for other purposes.

What then is the purpose of giving?

The principles of God are the opposite of the world. The world says, "get what you can and can what you get." God says, "Give and it shall be given unto you." What are some of the reasons that we give to God.

1. That our needs might be met. Philippians 4:16-19
2. That the needs of the saints might be met.
   2 Corinthians 9:9, 11-12
3. That the storehouse (the local church) might be adequately equipped. Malachi 3:8-10

4. That we might develop responsible attitudes.

1 Corinthians 16:1-2

The Bible teaches that we should make God the priority in our giving, above everything else. We are to give to Him the first fruits of all our increase. Exodus 23:19, Leviticus 23:10, Proverbs 3:9-10. These verses indicate that we are to give even before our total gross income is known. You can influence your total harvest by the amount of seed that you plant.

Where then is the place to give?

You don't collect your groceries from Coles and pay for them at Woolworths! Your first responsibility in giving is to the local church, it is the place where you are fed. Your giving to the local church is used in the following ways: -

1. To support the ministry. 1 Corinthians 9:1-14
2. To support visiting ministry. 3 John 1:5-8
3. To support missions. Romans 10:14-15, 2 Corinthians 11:7-9
4. To support local needs by sharing and caring.

2 Corinthians 8:9-15

Tithing (10% of gross income- salary) was God's standard under the old Covenant, it had its roots in the actions of Abraham when he tithed (gave one tenth) of the spoils of war to Melchizedek.

Genesis 14:18-20

In the New Covenant giving is a ministry that goes beyond that which was required under the law, sometimes beyond your apparent resources. God will supply abundantly as you are obedient to Him in this area. Philippians 4:19. God asks us to be generous. 2 Corinthians 9:5-11,

In Society

1 Peter 2:13-21 Notice we are to submit to the laws of man, employers etc. not for the law's sake but for the Lord's sake.

Romans 13:1-3 The word of God is quite clear about our submission in society. It is a means of demonstrating the life of Christ to others.

REVIEW LESSON 9

A NEW LIFESTYLE

1. What is the difference between an offering and a total sacrifice?
   _____
   _____

2. What is the difference between blind obedience and submission?
   _____
   _____

3. What is one practical way you can demonstrate submission in your living environment?
   _____
   _____

4. What does the following verse teach regarding submission in the local church? Hebrews 13:17
   _____
   _____

5. As a Christian how do you demonstrate submission as an employee?
   _____
   _____

6. State in your own words the principle of seedtime and harvest as found in 2 Corinthians 9:6.

7. What does Joshua 1:8 teach concerning prosperity?

8. What can we learn about the ministry of giving for every believer from 2 Corinthians 9:7?

9. Who should you submit to according to Ephesians 5:21?

10. If you seek first God's Kingdom, what will God do for you? Matthew 6:33

LESSON 10 THE CHURCH

WHAT IS THE CHURCH?

The church is not a building made of bricks, wood, stone, glass and steel. That is only the place where the church meets.

Colossians 1:18 The church is all born again people, described in several places in the New Testament as a body with Jesus as its head.

We are baptised into this body by the Holy Spirit 1 Corinthians 12:13 (note this is not referring to water baptism or baptism in the Holy Spirit but a baptism by the Holy Spirit into the body of Christ - this takes place at new birth - being born again.)

If we belong to Christ, we are all members of the one body, Christ is the head. We are members of the church of the Lord Jesus Christ.

The Bible talks about a local church as a group of born-again people meeting together in a local area.

The local church is cared for by a pastor (bishop or shepherd - these terms are synonymous). The purpose of the local church is to help Christians grow spiritually, you will have fellowship with other believers there and have opportunities to serve and encourage them as well as be encouraged by them.

It is important to attend a local church where God's Word is believed and preached for it will, teach you, reprove you, correct you and instruct you in righteousness. 2 Timothy 3:16

Let us not give up meeting together, as some are in the habit of doing, but let us encourage one another - and all the more as you see the Day approaching. Hebrews 10:24-25

It is important for you, for the local church and for the entire Body of Christ that you be committed to a local church to help it with your time, talents and finances.

The local church provides the four essential things for your Christian growth.

Acts 2:42 Teaching, Fellowship, Communion, Prayer.

Ephesians 4:11-12 Jesus Christ has put gifts within the church, apostles, prophets, evangelists, pastors and teachers, to perfect the saints, to do the work of the ministry. Philippians 1:1 Bishops (pastors) and deacons.

1 Thessalonians 5:12-13, Hebrews 13:17 tells us how we should treat them, Think highly of them and give them your wholehearted love because they are straining to help you. 1 Timothy 5.17 treat them with double honour.

Believers ought to hold regard for their fellow believers as better than themselves (Philippians 2:3) and remain in unity (Romans 15:5-6) so that we will fulfil Jesus prayer for us (John 17:20-23) and his great commission to us (Matthew 28:18-20).

Find out what your local church stands for, what is its vision and plan for the future, especially in your area. Is there something that you can do to assist the church in this. Ask your pastor or leader.

(For the pastor or leader taking this study with a group or an individual, this is a good place to share the vision of your local congregation.)

REVIEW LESSON 10

THE CHURCH

1. Acts 2:42-47 How did the early Christians respond to the nurture and fellowship they enjoyed?

2. What is the local church?

3. What is the Body of Christ?

4. What are four essential things the church provides for your Christian growth? Acts 2:42

5. What officers has the Lord appointed over the local church? Philippians 1:1

6. What gifts has the Lord given to his church? Ephesians 4:11

7. What is the purpose of these ministry gifts? Ephesians 4:12

8. What will the true pastor do for his congregation? Jeremiah 3:15

9. Now you have made a commitment to the Lord Jesus Christ He has included you in His body, have you now made a commitment to a local church in your time, talent and finances?

10. What task has Jesus committed to His church? Matthew 28:18-20

What Christian leaders around the world are saying about "The Foundations."

I wish to endorse fully the wonderful subjects for new believers by Howard Sands. These great truths are not only able to assist new Christians but will also help those who have been Christians for a period of time. They are basic and foundational, use them with utmost confidence.

Apostle Cliff Beard

Apostle to the Nations

Mildura, Victoria, Australia

It is so important for new Christians to be grounded in God's word. This booklet does that. The most prominent thing about this resource is the absolute reliance upon the word of God as "sincere milk" for those who have just been born again.

Tom Rawls

Senior Minister, Proclaimers

Norwich, UK

It is always good to see printed material being produced for brand new Christians. Howard Sands has presented us with such material to help new Christian believers get established in their walk with God.

Rodney W. Francis

Founder/Director, The Gospel Faith Messenger Ministry
Frmr leadership Team of Elim Churches of NZ
Paraparaumu, New Zealand

This is the prayer of thousands of servants of God who are in the discipling ministry. We look for a book to place in the hands of a new convert that will tell him, 'What to do now?' There is no book on this subject in the book stores. But now here is the prayer answered. I hope and trust that the soul winners will use this. We would like to see this book in the Indian languages.

Dr. P.G. Vargis

Founder/President, Indian Evangelical Team
New Delhi, India

Having known Pastor Howard Sands for over thirty Years and working closely with him in Outreach work I consider His teachings exemplary and of great importance to the church at large

Pastor Roy Hullah

Break-free Ministries Inc
Ministry Leadership, Gateway International
Adelaide, South Australia

"The Foundation" by Howard Sands is one of the best concise training tools for new believers I have ever seen. First the teaching is Biblical and supportive of Evangelical-Full Gospel teaching in its teaching on important doctrines, such as repentance, baptism by immersion and the baptism of the Holy Spirit with the evidence of speaking in tongues. Secondly, the various questions with the correlating Bible verses in the reviews will help the new believer to really understand and experience these important foundational truths.

Pastor Dennis Balcombe

Senior Pastor, Revival Christian Church
Founder and Director, Revival Chinese Ministries International
Kwai Chung, Hong Kong

An excellent and useful tool to help new Christians.

Rev Dr Ken Chant,

Founder, Vision International College
St Marys, NSW, Australia

I have known Pastor Howard Sands for over 25 years, he is a solid faithful Christian, and I can recommend this study booklet to be used by new Christians and believers. The chapters I believe are tailor made subjects, they are concise and to the point and will give a biblical foundation to those who study it.

Pastor Wayne Lyons

Senior Pastor, High Street Church.
Regional Chaplain Chaplaincy Australia, Chaplain to Veterans and 1WayFM Radio
Queanbeyan, NSW, Australia

"This easy to read and teach foundation series is a must for local churches and ministries. This foundation series reflects the extensive ministry and missionary experience of Howard and Joy Sands."

Apostle Leslie Munsamy
Founder/ President, Global Apostolic Centre
Chairman, Apostolic Fellowship of South Africa
Regional Director, Jesus for Africa Crusade
Frmr Principal, G.L.E.A.M Bible College
Durban, Kwa-Zulu Natal, South Africa

Bible based, endorsing the foundation for new and existing believers. User friendly, sending disciples forth to infect the world with rumours of resurrection.

Ray Buckingham
President - Sevenoaks Chapter, UK
Full Gospel Business Men's Fellowship International
Formerly, National Director over UK and Irish Republic
Tonbridge, Kent, UK

This is an inspirational Biblical teaching of God's word to equip and edify the saints, believers in His Vineyard, for an expansion of God's Kingdom on Earth... Hallelujah.

Rev Peter Kekere
Senior Pastor and Founder,
Christ Apostolic Church Praise Centre Incorporated
Director, International Praise Ministries
Bankstown, NSW, Australia.

There are many books available today written expressly for new Christians but none quite like this one. This short book tells it 'as it is'. It is hard hitting and easy to read and it is designed to develop a deep hunger for God in the new disciple and an enthusiasm to fulfil the great commission. It is also scripturally sound and uncompromising in its challenge. These are demanding days and we need to produce followers of Jesus who can withstand the increasing pressures of such 'end time' realities. Scripture asks... 'when He comes will He find faith on the earth?'

This book can be a tool to help us make sure the answer is in the affirmative.

Howard Barnes (Servant Apostle)
Co-founder and Co-director of The Call2Come
Truro, Cornwall, UK

As a resource, this book would be great for group work. Then with its questions it becomes a useful workbook and reference afterwards. As such, it will be valuable to assist in the discipleship of new Christians.

Rev Kevin Hovey
Director, Global Training Ministries,
Chester Hill, NSW, Australia

I am glad I read it and it was so encouraging for the new believers and has a very good foundation for those starting in salvation since it laid a good start.

Pastor Frederick Morara Mogere,
Pastor, Apostolic Church of America, Kenya Mission,
Kisii, Kenya.

I think you have produced a very helpful resource here. It is simple yet comprehensive and tackles each basic discipleship area with wisdom yet simplicity. I think the questions are very helpful indeed. I don't think there is anything that I would add or subtract.

Pastor Brian Medway

Senior Pastor, Grace Christian Fellowship
Leader, Canberra Pastors' Network,
Chairman, Crosslink Christian Network.
Canberra, ACT, Australia

It is vitally important for new Christians to receive instruction on the foundations of the faith to give them confidence and stability in their new walk. This little book gives an excellent summary of the major issues and will be a big help to new converts and also to enquirers.

Pastor Dennis Prince

Kingston City Church, Melbourne.
Director, Resource Christian Music
Melbourne, Victoria, Australia

This is a balanced and relevant material for the Body of Christ. It's instructive and informative!!! God Bless you Howard. You are a Blessing!

Dr. Ben Christopher Don

Senior minister, Higher Height Christian Embassy.
President, Global Covenant Minister's Network. [GCMN]
Kumasi, Ashanti Region, Ghana

The publication is great. The foundational truths that every believer needs to know regardless of how long you have known the Lord.

Pastor Kenny Bisha Goma
Senior Pastor, New Beginnings Christian Church
Kafue, Zambia

The Foundations - a study for new believers is an invaluable tool for new believers who want to grow in Christian faith. The subjects covered are significant to one with a longing heart to grow in the word. It gives you a foundation for you to build upon and can also be used by bible teachers for new believers, so use this classic study as a bible study guide.

Bishop Dr. Gerishon K. Njoroge
The founder and the presiding Bishop,
Wings of Life Gospel Centre Churches,
Kenya Director, Citadel of Hope School
National Chairman, Communion of Christian Churches, Kenya
Nairobi, Kenya

The teaching in this important booklet is simply laid out and easy to understand. Howard has done an exceptional job in taking the essential truths contained within the Word of God and making them palatable for the new Christian's early understanding.

Pastor Eric Roggeveen
Frmr Senior Pastor, Riverlands Christian Church
Frmr Blue Mountains District Leader, Australian Christian Churches.
Penrith, NSW, Australia

I don't know of any basic guide to establishing new Christians in their faith in Christ that answers every question. Whoever takes their relationship with a new Christian seriously, will realize this and respond as the Holy Spirit leads, not as a book dictates. However, this study informs a follower's faith with the Word, touching on the areas of life, that are foundational to an ongoing walk of growth and fruitfulness in the Kingdom. Howard accomplishes his goal of laying a foundation.

Captain Dale Brooks
Team leader, Capricorn Region Salvation Army
Rockhampton, Queensland, Australia

I have personally known Ps Howard Sands for over 16 years and his Foundations Course is very Biblically based, straight forward and to the point, easy to read, study and understand for new believers and seekers alike. The review sections are very helpful and insightful.

This short but balanced course will enrich, encourage, strengthen and empower new believers and longer standing believers/seekers as well.

I recommend this scripture, meaty and Jesus/Bible based course to any individual and church/bible study group. Ps Howard's love for Jesus, The Word of God and for new believers to be well grounded is very clear. Well done Ps Howard and thank you for your passion.

Maurice Antonelli
Go Global-Director
OG Baptist Church-Missions
Geelong, Victoria, Australia

Howard has covered all the subjects new converts need to understand to go onto maturity.

Rev Tony Rawson
Itinerant Bible Teacher
Melbourne, Victoria, Australia

Howard Sands has written a succinct but comprehensive foundation studies that will help new believers to lay a strong foundation for their on-going discipleship. His combination of both didactic as well as inductive approach makes this foundation study series very effective for new believers.

Rev Benny Ho
Senior Pastor, Faith Community Church,
Founder of Arrows School of Ministry
Coordinator of Australian-Asian Churches Network
Committee Member of the Love-Singapore Network
Perth, Western Australia, Australia

This booklet has been very well prepared by Howard to enable new believers to become established in the faith. It is a brief presentation of the first principles in the life and growth of the Christian, yet it is certainly thorough and concise. Church leaders will benefit by the use of this short, but extensive manual, as they seek to extend the Kingdom.

Pastor John W. J. Hewitt
Apostolic Church Australia
Frmr National Leader/President 1980-84
Pioneer missionary in Papua New Guinea Highlands 1962-70
Senior Minister Highway Christian Church Knox Vic 1970-98

Founding member & past chairman, Australian Pentecostal Fellowship

Knox, Melbourne, Victoria, Australia

This is good materials especially for new believers.
Pastor Eliah Edward Mauza

Senior Pastor, Endtime Harvest Church, Lifeway Ministries International

Apostle, Chairman of Pastors Fellowship in Dodoma,

Founder of African Task Mission Network,

Dodoma, Tanzania

The booklet is concise and gives a firm foundation to new Christians in their new-found faith. It is easy to read and clearly explains all the jargon in plain English. It fills the believer with hope and assurance whilst equipping them for their new life. It teaches them to focus on God and to seek guidance from his word. A very good booklet.
Pastor Paul Hutchinson

Associate Pastor, Church of The Rock,

Kingswood, NSW, Australia

This publication is timely for church leaders who want to see their congregation grow in the Lord and ready for the return of the Lord. I recommend it to all Pastors, Leaders and Missionaries.
Rev Franklin Andrew Koroma,

Founder and General Overseer, Living Word Ministries,

Freetown, Sierra Leone.

I found the book, "The Foundations," as a must use book for our newcomer's foundation classes, that will lead to water baptism. My church is now using the book for our newcomers/baptismal class, so I wish to recommend it to church leaders for their church's foundation class use.

Bishop Godspower E. Adaka

General overseer/founder

Covenant of Grace Bible Church Int'l Inc.

Presiding Bishop: Anointed Bishops International Fellowship,

Africa Regional Overseer, Global Church Fellowship International,

Africa Continental Bishop, International Fellowship of Independent Interdenominational Churches and Christian Ministries.

Benin City, Edo State, Nigeria

About Howard Sands

Passionately wanting see you come to personally know Christ and live the overcoming life, Howard's aim is to lift you from where you are in your experience to where God says you are in His Word. He wants you to be empowered to make a difference in your world. He takes teams to minister in power packed evangelistic and leadership events across 26 nations encompassing every continent.

Rev. Dr. Howard Sands, is Founder/International Director of Beautiful Feet Task Force (BFTF). They specialise in showing ministers how to transform their churches to radically change their communities into places where people want to live and positively influence their world. Their philosophy is simple, they believe the church members should be seen as the church in the community. What makes them unique is that they show leaders how to build maturity in the church, unity between churches and create confidence in their members to influence their world.

With his wife Joy, the delight of his life, they are often found enjoying the Australian beach or bush when refreshing from the demands of itinerant ministry. It was the challenges of pioneering/pastoring Australian churches in Canberra and Sydney that led Howard to take his passion for developing people into overcomers, into publicly available material to impact more people for change. Howard has also been privileged to be part of planting around 20 churches through crusade evangelism in India. He has degrees in Business Management/ Marketing, Ministry and a Doctor of Divinity. Since 1996 Howard & Joy have enjoyed living at the foot of Sydney's Blue Mountains with their now adult, two married children, and love doting on their grandchildren.

Endorsement captions

I wish to endorse fully the wonderful subjects for new believers by Howard Sands.

Apostle Cliff Beard

It is so important for new Christians to be grounded in God's word. This booklet does that.

Pastor Tom Rawls

I hope and trust that the soul winners will use this.

Dr. P.G. Vargis

"The Foundations" by Howard Sands is one of the best concise training tools for new believers I have ever seen...."

Pastor Dennis Balcombe

An excellent and useful tool to help new Christians.

Rev Dr Ken Chant,

This easy to read and teach foundation series is a must for Local Churches and ministries.

Apostle Leslie Munsamy

Bible based, endorsing the foundation for new and existing believers.

Ray Buckingham

As a resource, this book would be great for group work.

Rev Kevin Hovey

It is simple yet comprehensive and tackles each basic discipleship area with wisdom yet simplicity.

Pastor Brian Medway

This is a Balanced and Relevant material for the Body of Christ.

Dr. Ben Christopher Don

www.ingramcontent.com/pod-product-compliance
Lightning Source LLC
Chambersburg PA
CBHW050320010526
44107CB00055B/2323